All the Peaches &
Mangoes I Would
Sell For You.

Ivy Ngugi *(Ngōgee)*

she/her

POE023010   POETRY / Subjects & Themes / Death, Grief, Loss
LCO019000   LITERARY COLLECTIONS / Women Authors

ISBN: 978-1-7370428-3-9 Paperback
LCCN: 2021907458

First print edition July 2021.

Illustrations by Anjali Singh. Illustrations in *Running, Solitaire,* and *All the peaches and mangoes that I would sell for you* done by Ivy Ngugi.

Ivyprintsllc.com

Choose love, always.

PROVERBS 16:18

Love's gonna get you killed, but pride's gonna be the death of you

Because if you are killed in love's name, passion will flow out your bleeding corpus into the world

Outliving your murmuring heart's last encore

Being killed by what you love ensures that at least one person, place, or thing will feel your absence in passing breezes

Dying in pride guarantees solo smokey afterlife; you were born into man's community of fiery heat, but you fanned your flame so high

Swallowing them whole because you swore you were the sun.

Your pride killed communities of men in love and through that loveloss tragedy they will be remembered.

In your selfish deed you will be forgotten- pride finally claiming what belongs to him

Because when self-righteous villains fall out of self created struggle and off DIY pillar heights, kingdoms do not weep

Prideful deaths cannot be undone; you cannot command pillars to fall the way men do

Fallen angel men must choose to fly off four sided granite standings without wings and embrace ground's loving pain

Pride traps you on four sided pillar heights because you fear meeting pain's precise promise at the finish line

You'll remain on your two squared feet wishing you could summon those same wings that brought you to these heights

Pride's python constriction slithers in brain sulci promising no love awaits prideful men below so why risk pain in the name of a forgotten grave? Why take accountability for your false fightings when no one will be there to hear apologetic sorry?

If love was there to remedy and kill python's poison, you would fall freely knowing those four sides aren't forever

And while your apologies may not travel to those who survived your carnage

Your stain on mother earth's granite counter will be seen by all

All things have punctual period endings on this great green globe.

If love was there to remedy python's prideful poison, you would fall because pain's assurance isn't louder than freedom's bellowing welcome home

New love awaiting you in the next sentence.

Originator

Same hands that cupped my mother's breasts so tenderly carefully and deliberately pummel into my chest, breaking the heart of two joined souls

Lips that once carried sweet nothings into her awaiting ear now curl downwards

Cursing my uncontrollable existence; reminding me of how I plague your once happy life

With every scoff and exasperated sigh, your unspoken emotions bleed to the surface- showing not telling how little I really mean to you

Never an I love you too sincere or a pat on the back too validating, to unite us into one

Arms that lifted Pompeii ruins and Olympus stamped soles now grow

Tired at the thought of inspiring happiness from the ruin all around me

You bravely trampled wheat grass to settle the picnic of her dreams atop newly fallen floras.

Nowadays, your foot only grows excited for the new low you will personally walk me to

A heart once created from the raw fruits of passion

Beats a depressing muffled love song from the world's tiniest violin

Maestro of my never ending numbness, you'll meet me at opus 21 this year

Arranging the happy clefts in my voice to balance your orchestra's lonesome crotchet

And believe me I know, I exist as everything you never wanted.

You don't see her in me

Your heart clings to the truth that I am a living reminder that she is not here.

Are you hungry?

I am starving

Food is scarce

My stomach aches

The sand is barren

I haven't eaten since yesterday

Mouths empty for 3 generations, raised to the sky awaiting blessing showers

And it was at breakfast, I had fruit and rice cake

Like pretty little birds we flock

To wash it down I drank vanilla protein shake

Migrating wherever the next meal is promised

For dinner I think I'll go get a cut of ribeye, the most perfect steak

Never setting in one place like the sun, our solace paid in recompense of porridge and naan

I asked for almond milk not soy, my mother's common mistake

And through my grateful feast, I smile at the bellow of the bowl thankful for the giving

But I guess, she'll give whatever and I'm willing to take.

Have You Seen Them?

Putting up missing posters only encourages

absence.

It inflates the confidence of the terrible thief who stole
your favorite lamp from your sacred tower.

Missing posters stand as warnings to the members of these
invisible societies

Each bulletin board posted with your profile, every power
line plugged with your description, entire billboards
advertising your last whereabouts.

But when you see these reminders from your remote
trapping, you can't help but feel a twinge of pain and
bitterness in your heart.

Here you are in all these places you'd never gone.

Missing posters only encourage absence because

When I'm reminded that I'm missing

I could never dream of returning to a place with a me sized
crater.

Because around that crater, is a failed resurgence of life

A new construction zone is trying to flourish.

There is wet cement that seems to never dry, trees that never grow past sap height, and grass that grows in sporadic patches.

These are the living failures that have spawned around my absence.

So much failure, so much stagnancy, such little progress to be made; It all started with you.

Because now more than ever, your loneliness is vast.

Your sadness jets in paper news; tears coloring the sky blue, reigning from sea to shining sea.

And while I do appreciate the gesture of looking, I still find it vain because the individual on newspapers is never to return. Who you'll find is the reincarnated soul of a body buried in invisible graveyards.

A statue of remembrance for all that's been lost.

Nam Saying

Nam saying? Life was so beautifully chaotic

Every decision made for us, we didn't ever have to think

Just do. Because they owned our minds, used our bodies as muscle, Nam saying? It was easy because we just were; inhibitors of flesh, residents to this body

Steel rimmed Chevy ventricles pumping out American glory to thirsty vena cavas

Bullets branding American stars of bravery and courage, it's a blessing to do this. Nam Saying?

My strong Chevy muscle seeping my red, white, and blue

I see it not as a loss, but rather a sacrifice

May my blue American banner, red Yankee blood, and white all knowing stars fertilize the soil

Eliminating Marx's weeds, long after our departure

Vi et the design of Lady Liberty, that we patriots bring back victory and not shame. Nam saying?

Free

Thick globs ------ narrow streams, steady

rhythm.

Increase pace with violent rapids at source.

S l o w i n g   w i t h   g e n t l e   c a l m s

t h a t   f o l l o w   w i t h   *rapids.*

Cascading down, love laced saline streams
aspire to grow a garden

so rich and green that the legacy of tears shall be
history long erased

How Insensitive

I am the physical reminder to these two married people

of the feelings they cannot enact on.

A buffer between acidic adultery and basic loyalty, I
wedge myself- the equilibrium to those too friendly
gazes-

at the door of possible curiosities

Firmly and steadily I guard the opportunistic doorway of
things that can not be undone.

I am the physical reminder to these two married people,

that although their fleeting moments combine to hours of
cinematic gushing

that their moments are just that. Clipped and unremoved
from the rest of the day-

irrelevant in the grand scheme of things.

You are not a mosaic,

you will not combine your lonesome tiles to produce an
explanation for your emotions.

But you are allowed your sweet passing hello's, rising chuckles from your bellows, and setting goodbyes 'til the next morning arise.

I am the physical reminder to these two married people that they can dabble in

encouraging greetings and playful banter.

Lest that banter transform into ubiquitous dialogue, breathing life into your day,

I will be here, standing beside you.

The physical reminder of the vows you swore to your two married partners.

Isla Mujeres

You prayed to God I'd still be here

Just so you could bless someone else

Melting into melancholy, I moped bitterly
For the first time realizing the vastness of our island
without you present

You carried my beach, because sand never vanishes

A confident woody row boat sat tethered to palm tree's
base; existing for emergencies that would require
immediate evacuation if paradise was lost

Rushing into the ocean, we would abandon each other and
abandon ecosystem corruptions that awaited in swaying
palm tree prophets

Waving goodbye forever to ember islands of happiness
past, letting foam float us apart onto new shores.

Paradise puzzle was still intact when you took your corner
pieces without say.

But see, I'm with you always

Underfoot, my love's grainy residue prick and marry into
your soles, divorcing you away

You're welcome, my love fuels you even away from me

Even while you row towards uncertainty, you will still find pieces of me pocketed in shorts because that is my assurance. Twenty grains poorer, but my beach doesn't show it.

Where does a lost woman sing for love on an island meant for two?

Shuddering Cameras

Blink, blink, blink - hand raises

Snap, snap, shutter

Captured.

Every second of the day held hostage in our four sided lobes

New memories, where oh where will you go? Stop, don't go- don't vanish

Fingers swiping frantically trying to savor this moment

NO, STOP, NO, NO, NO, remember me. Please?

Sunny beach day drinking mangorita

Lila's hand stretches outward lazily

Baby's laugh oceans clash sand hot to touch

Scene goes dark.

NO, STOP, come get me!

Baby's laugh echoes to the sky expansively haunting as
ever

Lila too. Her too red cheeks go pale

Sand to snow, waves stop

Finger hovers, reminiscing for the future

Tap, lights out.

God Complex

Oh my, it must be so lonely being you. I mean- even God has company

Holy Spirit I know you're not with him

And oh, Prince of Peace, the chaos he invites cannot be a home to you.

So I implore you, how lonely is it? Because even God has company, company that exalts His every footstep and a choir that rejoices at every breath

You say you're so above, yet all you do is fall

in and out of self created struggle you refuse to acknowledge.

You say you're so above, yet all you do is fall

Out of cents, because you spend wit and dollars on climbing higher.

You can do no wrong, my self proclaimed deity because as the sole creator of all your chaos and desolate melancholy. You indeed are a God. Creator of problems big and small

Nothing glorious in your realm, only failure and deceit

And you sit above it atop it all because

you

are

a

KING.

And the only mistake kings make is accepting the
accidental fate of the heavy crown they must wear.

Do condoms come with rape?

looking down before me, I smirk with satisfaction

I knew i didn't need you to just for me to get some action

and just like you said, you are on contraception

my finesse- I slid it off with such discretion

the arch of your back- i'm absolutely mesmerized

the way your hips curve and bounce off me, the sensation has me hypnotized

i've done us a favor you see- connecting us by bonding our origins with raw authentic passion

you can't say you didn't like it- your back trembling and your toes contorting italicized.

you're welcome.

i've done us a favor you see- connecting us by bonding our origins with raw unfiltered passion.

not suppressing my love inside that glove, just for you to toss it in the bin

unfiltered and honest, that's how i'm fucking you.

my honesty growing inside of you more concrete and

final with each thrust until finally

20

we reach our climax.

focusing intently, i nurse your core with my honesty
-which is now *our* honesty- and you clench around me
as to absorb

                   every

                                  last

                                                  drop

in mutual agreement.

and although my honesty floats inside you, the
truth is unbeknownst to you, and it's my love that
makes me shoulder it for the both of us.

God Sent

Armed with religion, poisonous prejudice running through my veins

I rinse sin clean without choking on repentance

Allowing the lies that bubble from within a clean escape route to new truth.

This mouth is wiped clean of wrongdoing, forgiven for false fightings.

It spends seconds and four seasons reciting the dooming peril that is preserved for those who dare challenge its solid syllables.

Gnawing lust off the bones of love. Swallowing sex to secrete life. It is no easy thing to purify from within.

That is why I force myself to chug down sleazy and wash it down with dishonest tea.

And so quickly my black ashened knees fall prayer to the floor for white Jesus light to come and castrate the poisonous sin in which I swallowed pleasurably.

Chewing on Popeye's salvation biscuit, guzzling grape wine's true wrath, I conjure a storm of sickness from within to up chuck nauseating wrongdoings.

To newly introduce their potential, giving them the opportunity to be clean again.

Black Girl

Dear Black girl,

With your true earth skin mother to all- originator to all originators

I would scorch down this already melting earth to haul justice to your grave.

Like wax it will all sludge to the ground with purposeful malice.

The trees would weep their buckets of sap in honor of you- the sweetest gift of all.

And as their sap drowns out the clamour of violence, together in solidarity, they would scream as they lit themselves ablaze.

Flames licking burrowed insect homes, sparking dark cavern trunks.

Starting at firm roots, each ember and coal would multiply across the coarse bark till the tails of every twig and the plane of every leaf would combust in harmonious grief.

And the forests wouldn't stop, no. Let the oxygen that was perforated from your lungs be absent in availing smoky winds.

Hanging low on us all, let smoky black skies reign supreme; raping our lungs of the freedom you were robbed.

Let smoke and fiery destruction burn ablaze on every hilltop on which you frolicked and every mountainside you had yet to climb.

For you my truest love, I would sacrifice worlds over to ensure that soot permanently resides in the lungs of those who dared forget you.

For you I would let oceans go dry, and impregnate barren lands with drought.

For you I'd spend ten sleepless eternities to ensure your soul consolidates with peace to become whole.

My sweet little Black girl, there is not a sun I wouldn't extinguish, nor a beach I wouldn't sit upon, counting every grain of sand, watching you in the stars, waiting till you came home again.

longing

today i talked to my mom in the car

open conversation like the windows,

judgment blowing out the AC to be carried off by a breeze.

she held my hand and laughed at all the right times.

daughter.

easy smiles. I wish it was always like this

Intent

When I was just a budding flower, you came to my garden to fertilize me so that I may grow, and enamoured by the beauty of the blossoms around me, you saw my potential. There, snuggled in my warm roots, I watched and allowed you to tend to me and my every weed. I won't forget the gentleness veiled with intense concern you showed for me the first day. The way you delicately showered me with water, electrifying my veins sending refreshing sparkles to my core.

I was just a sprout when I welcomed your care- my shy two juvenile leaves erupting at your tender deliberate touch while nipping away weeds and unwanted distraction. I watched you as you worked so meticulously. And I too learned how to catch the drops of rain; I perfected the art of nipping my own dead leaves. I practiced while you were away- me alone in my garden trying to recreate the results of my master while I was still an apprentice. I grew from that tentative leaf sprout into a stem. No longer were my two leaves lonesome, they had multiplied and gathered a network of leaves along my stem. I was more than just a sprout and others could see it too. When you came to me that last appointment, night had fallen and the remnants of day slithered in my veins- blanketing me with safe nutrients. There you stood: pail in hand, ready to water, but my dampened soil revealed that I was nourished. You picked and prodded- gently as ever- at my many new leaves hoping to find purpose, but you found none. I was growing in your absence, and with your unhelpful nightly visit, I asked myself. What is the point- watering me only at night, when there is no light for me to bathe? Only lonesome chilly moon beams teasing at the next new day.

You could not water me because I was nourished, and you could not correct my weeds because there were none. So there you were, pail in hand, ready to water, incompetent as ever- because my purpose had outgrown you. So for all the days you left me alone, I was showering myself in adoration when one day a passerby grew enchanted with the way my stem pointed ambitiously towards the sky and entered the gates of my garden. Bewitched at the flawlessness of my technique, he gazed from the white border and entered the gates after five minutes of deliberating. When a looming shadow blanketed me in a chilly darkness, my leaves shuddered and leaned inwards; when I dared bare my virgin blossom to the now blocked sun, I was surprised to see a new face. In the place of a pail and clippers, sat a pot nestled by gloves and a small shovel in the opposite hand.

Welcome to my care.

Your work commenced, and your fingers moved with skillful pace. The shovel you held became acquainted with my rich soil- picking and prodding, tussling the old and the new soil. Tossing away malnutritious old soil and revitalizing it with herbal blessings, my roots were like new. The pot that sat in the crook of your elbow now presented itself in front of me in its rich clay glory, and my leaf twisted in confusion. I felt my foundations loosen, then and there and behold, you had carved a careful circular incision around me-you were uprooting me?

Panic swelled at the core of my roots; when I welcomed you to my care, this was not what I expected. I wanted pampering and new experience given to me so I could take that sweet knowledge and teach it to my roots. I wanted rejuvenation, timed satisfaction and endearing doting. I did not care to be uprooted by my grounds- to have my fetters broken and bared vulnerable. I cannot believe this! Oblivious to my anguish, you begin packing neighboring soil into the clay bellow to about halfway. Once you grew satisfied with your collected earth, your hands -cupped in maniacal prayer- started for my sacred grounds, specifically the holy perimeter you carved out.

I had nowhere to run to, so I resigned my qualms and accepted my doomed captivity. I had seen many a flora succumb to this same fate: a recklessly ambitious gardening apprentice rushing in with sharp tools pointing and dissecting our gentleness causing immediate wilting before the stem could reach their varying means of collecting- a pot, a plastic bag, clay bellows. I had seen it all. I didn't even get to flower, my virgin flora had yet to show the world the fruits of our hard work. Anguish meddled with the water in my veins bringing surreal dread to my core, preparing to lose it all. I cannot believe that in welcoming your care, I willfully sacrificed the fruit of my womb to a comfortable stranger. Your inviting tools piqued my leaves' interest, the excitement of discovery momentarily blinded my solitary vision. I cannot believe that for all the days I cared for myself in this grounding rich soil, I thought that newness was what

I needed. The promise of new experience was what I signed up for, and I trusted you because in your audacious covering of the sun, I felt shrouded. Sighing deeply, setting all complaints to the depths of mother earth, I began to accept death's suffocating grip just for it to never arrive. The moment your fingertips united to make a net between the earth and my roots, I was strongly clenching my furled blossom praying for reprieve, wincing for anticipating pain that never came. Your safety net executed your intentions because in your embrace, I felt at ease with myself and my blossom did not fall and wilt as I expected. Assigning a firm squeeze to my foundation, my flora was airborne and swiftly transplanted into the freshly fluffed soil that sat deep in the bellows of the clay opening. Your hands worked with surgical precision, agilely firming and packing the soil around me to anchor my stem in this new vessel, assuring me that no uprooting will soon concur with a last gentle pat and savory caress of my stem.

My leaves, shaken with survival adrenaline, started to set and sag comfortably- disobeying my frigid demeanor- sitting in their new comfort. My leaves only sat this way when they were being showered with nourishing water or lazing in the sun's warm glory, morphing the honey rays into sweetness that I could ingest. Burdened with stress, my blossom also began to consent to the unwillful fate of comfortable sagging because she too grew comfortable. When the last drop of dread evaporated from my furled core, I felt my peace return. Like fat rain droplets, it lingered- glopping and sludging its way to every vacuole and empty vein cavern in my system- welcoming too absent homeostasis.

Running

Men can be free and wave to anyone they pass

Their waning smile won't be taken as an invitation to
pervert their ass

Wading in and out of conversation- skillful butterflies

Waxing disrespect at its root, upon its introduction in
tone

Fully assured no new harm should befall them at their
verbal affirmation

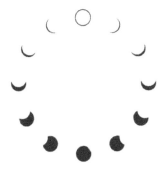

26 allegations; I know that's no mistake,

I ain't a mathematician, but I can do some calculating.

1 was a drunk night and forgotten manners

2 was because you dumped shame, manners, and respect at the gates of your mother's womb. 3 was because your belt was too tight around the groin, and you had to let it breathe.

4-8 because why the hell not. Although an understatement, it is quite a privilege to be touched by you.

9 because how dare she deny you of your pleasure. You grab what you want

10 because the last one ruined your mojo, and the groove cannot go disturbed.

11 was a repeat of 1. You were clearly too drunk, too stupefied to summon the strength required to pin someone in place.

12 was the reason you stopped it for a while.

13 needed to know how good she was making you feel

14 was a must because the way those legs were looking, they were ready to run off

15 and 16 technically didn't happen. Locker room talk means nothing without athletic execution

17 was because your fingers needed a stress ball substitute to squeeze away the anxiety.

18 you accept because this was your rapist adultification; you are matured.

19 and 20, "No I didn't." You make no effort to disguise the disgust that paints itself clear in the paper planes of your face upon hearing the salacious slander that dares to ruin your great name.

How dare they forcibly penetrate their broken narratives on your innocent action?

21 through 26 didn't happen because you refuse to dig so terribly deep into your memory to recall maybe moments in your history that were everything short of memorable.

You've stopped listening, but maybe -*just* maybe-you'll tune in when the count reaches 45.

You'll walk into that 45th office ready to face that allegation. Re-charged and erect, because that's a position you like.

So you see, a girl has no president; what she has is a man. Whose fathers before him passed down the precedent that power was found between her two legs

And through the executive order directly passed down from God, he assumed his birthright to raid her tombs. Fisting power from her chalice, it was his right to wield her key.

A girl has no president; what she has is a key that unlocks every door before her own.

Pimp Pimp V.1

Pimp pimp, hooray!

Pimp pimp, hooray!

My pimp blue suit saves the day

Pimp blue suit, always preaching 'bout salvation

Claiming that we're His, but it's you who's always taking

Say He's the one who saves, but when the butt of your glorious gilded cane meets the plates of my skull

I remember that I am indeed at your mercy.

Pimp blue suit, always preaching about salvation

You bring me to His alter to rejoice at your saving

Because it was you, right?

Who saved me from His otherwise cruel destiny

It was you who saved me from giving it up for free. Save the reoccurring occasions I can't save myself from you.

Overwhelmed by your divinity, how could I begin to block my blessing?

I could not and would not; because even if I did, how dare I rebel against he who saves

Rescued me from normalcy, I failed to do it for myself.

He who wanted me to give it up for free, watched as my free was plundered.

Watched them, as they bartered and bickered over what high currency they would purchase to fuel them for my ravaging up ahead.

Too broken and too tired to object, I let my quiet freedom replenish their deafening lust.

Sitting mighty on His throne, was I meant to cower for salvation? Beg for rescuing from this handpicked destiny?

All so you can call me ungrateful: I refuse to cower and crow. I should've been enough for saving.

Blue clad blessing, my pimp in his superhero cape

he is ever present and merciful.

I see him three times a day, and his teal chariot always looms at the street corner

My ears perk up at the slight introduction of treble from his closed mouth

he doesn't make me give it up for free, except when he does.

his currency is green, and it's the green that I need.

Green and blue, I love my peacock pimp.

Solitaire

When a queen looks down at her deck of cards, does she feel her life staring back up at her?

Her one two many children, sprade around three country in various manors and castles.

Fruits of her womb, they baked in her warm oven

Only to be grabbed by mongering customers upon golden crusting at their ready completion.

Her heart spread in so many directions, each chamber filled with varying queen mother worries.

Tucked between ring and middle finger, joker's mischievous contortion leaps off its white plain surface

Landing in her majesty's pupil, twisting her brain silly with goofy memory.

Inconspicuously, the corner of her mouth winds upward remembering the jokes and happy moments shared with her closest confidant.

Lucky diamond seven sits at the heart of her spread

Reestablishing the favor and good fortune that sit perched on her gilded fingers.

How often is it that when she sees K for King her fingers linger when grazing the plain paper surface?

How often does palm itch for his secure grip?

Quietly observant and silver tongued, K reminds her of the uniting peace her ace provides to all he meets.

And when she locks eyes with her soulless paper tethered, does she feel the weight of motherhood start to expand in her womb?

Does she momentarily reduce herself to just a container?

Ready and waiting to be impregnated with tens, nines, eights, and beyond.

Definition of Queen Mother.

Dementia

How does one remember to be racist?

How *does* one remember to hate?

When black pants look grey and white is too bright

How does the mind somersault twenty years backwards
then tomorrow fall splat like four year old cartwheels?

You remember to hate Black, but forget your shadow is
your own and that skies darken daily.

White comes as comfort, yet your two forgotten
daughters will say otherwise

Insisting you've blackened their existence with a cloak of
dementia

They too hate Black, but for a different reason.

Ma'am Your Daughter Wasn't Raped

sighing really softly, you caress the glass corner,

such tender affection written identically across the planes of your face and depth of the photo- a now faint memory.

bright bulbous eyes wide and unafraid captivate you.

she is sitting perched on a black patio chair; chin proud and stout daring the camera to look away. it was her birthday.

evidence of frosting sat caked in the corners of her mouth painted deliberately on her right cheek.

she was seven, this was the biggest she'd ever been and she stopped everyone to reinstate this declaration.

white with winter joy, her christened teeth remain confined to a stubborn pout.

you cling to this final missing piece of innocence. another year gone just like that.

forever, this is how you'll remember her.

Knock knock- a set of knuckles rapping at the door. You make your way down to the door to calm its aggressors.

Once it's opened, two uniformed men appear to be the door's harassers.

Bewilderment blankets your features causing the main abuser of the door to speak, and her name is

the first thing to tumble off his lips and fall into your heart filling you with dread.

We're here to report that there has been an incident. She has tragically, but successfully managed to lure a victim to perform unspeakable things.

She has defiled and corrupted the victim, stripping them of their honor and worth.

She says she was raped, but ma'am your daughter wasn't raped. Her smouldering bright eyes and dramatic lashes thrashed wildly in the wind singling out her unassuming prey.

Ma'am, your daughter wasn't raped, her stubborn pout was slashed with rogue and quivered cleverly at anyone naive enough to find themselves ensnared in her christened white jaws.

She wasn't raped because when we found her, her legs spoke kumbaya: a neglected Christmas gift wrapped in denim waiting for an embrace from any passerby.

Wide and inviting just like her extroverted neckline, a warm friendly greeting from her breasts inside her clothes which were missing the embrace and protection of a bra.

His arm extends out to knead my tense shoulder and he flashes a reassuring smile

Ma'am, your daughter wasn't raped, but she's paid her fee

for womanhood.

Goldi's Locs

I've got a million dreads locced up in this head of mine

Staying prisoner to a heart that yells inside a soundproof set of lips; these locs spin no gold

Only gilding problems in prosperity, creating expensive solutions.

Mind memorizing chores, everyday feeling like Monday

Everyday waking, mercilessly manifesting Friday freedoms only to be squashed by Thursday's thumb of almost without A & M

I'm yearning for yesterday when in fact it is so far.

Two hours equals history and a day is monumental.

Both standing for forever, becoming slowly forgotten by the thoughts that erected their existence

When water shrinks weary and time grows tired I will rest.

But today I will play in this game rigged perfectly for two

Been Away

When I was pregnant with her, you dribbled my feelings up and down the court

Careless of the stress I endured trying to keep up with you two.

Your orange cheeky mistress, scant clothing leaving little to the imagination; her narrow black stripe dressing outlines the forms of her round figure

Her round figure that your hands so tenderly touched. Lingering seconds longer than your goodbye embrace.

She was your mistress, this orange cheeky woman.

You'd leave me alone in our shared bed, in a house we bought together

To keep her company in the rented out arena, that meant nothing to me.

You'd layup with her while leaving me open and vulnerable

No cover from opposing slam dunks.

Three points for effort, a free throw just to lock in victory

That's all I want from you; more effort.

On the road while you're away, she's in your right embrace and not me

Treating her like a superstar rookie, neglecting me like a water boy

You make me feel like this final's ring is no more than a forgettable basket

Club 27

I can't make geometric arguments with someone who
chooses to be this obtuse

You're a little cute, but not enough to proof your
incorrect point that I'm outlying.

You said you'd never committed arson

But the way your lies licked and lit me whole,

I never would've gassed it.

Every lie spoken signals orange gaslightings my mind's
odometer

Fueling this descent into new vulnerability

My sadness stretches into first position hanging low like
my downward dog you banished because he barked too
boldly for your quiet oasis.

I know no nirvana in my mind's winehouse because I'm
too drunk off your stench

And too sick from poison laced love sweet wine.

You color my world in splotchy red wine hues, never
gifting rose colored vision.

You, creator of my personal hell, that is childhood cherry
scented

Only you could stand a pretty girl's tears because you
love making me cry

18 with 27 issues you have got to get some help

Because I am not Abel, to stand your insistent Caining

And am not brother to keep your deepest sorrows

My strength has no scent, but my weakness is repugnant
and dominates your narrow nose holes.

I wonder blindly

Third eye glued shut, deaf to internal dialogue

Cerberus, my only guide and emotional support dog

Gnaws on my limbs as he walks me

Around the four walled pen you've built to keep me
prisoner

You won't let me grow.

You're 18 with 27 issues

Nine issues too advanced in this series that's hardly
complete

I asked for you not knowing your baggage

So I guess it's my fault if I remain in this airport without
service

Waiting for a flight to never come

Beautiful: Sold for $10k

Because I'm such a man, I'll start to spend your money like a woman.

Is that what you want to see?

Breaking each masculine block wall down with green dollar hammers and steely nickel drills.

Spend till there's man no more

Spend till you have no more

Because by then it won't matter.

My piggy bank belly, once filled with dead green savings,

Will have long since been spent on adequate femininity.

Steely nickels will be diamonds and green dead men are swapped for mortal glimmering emeralds.

It'll have been spent so well, that when you reach into your linen lined pocket, you won't mind its barrenness.

Because your daughter is baroness quality.

She is woman enough to reap the fruits of chivalry.

Including its poisonous fruits of violence; femininity over flowered, so all can pluck as they please.

This is what you wish

To have a dandelion daughter

Whose wishes float into the expansive nothing sky

By the stifling grip of another.

And because I am no fool, I will accept the generous accommodations of your wallet.

But be warned, I will spend your money like a woman, doting on all things fine and refined.

But I will be selfish like the dead green men you spent so long before.

Just For Me

Yes, it's just for me.

Sitting on the toilet, waiting to be pretty

My roots, my roots, oof the growth kicked in

Thankful to my mother for the gifts of growth embedded in my genes

A story in four parts, I'll let my sectioned hair tell it.

Part 1/4:

Upon applying the cool petroleum protectant at the perimeter of my scalp and in the lines of the four sections on my head

The moisturizing goop melts and christens my dome greasy, protecting my skin and scalp from the incoming fire.

Removing the box from the bag, my eyes find my pretty little friend's on the box and all my follicles cringe together in excitement, knowing what was about to transpire

It's been way too long

I gush to our new growth

No worries, these kinks will be straightened out soon and we'll emerge beautiful. Out mother's bathroom salon

Handing me the comb, mother instructs me to thoroughly rake through any tangles and unwind complex knots, to avoid irreversible hair loss.

Please be more gentle

My strands plea to my heavy hand, I know I'm not tender headed, but while in my mother's stomach, my follicles absorbed her sensitivity

And my scalp her stubbornness.

Ouch, that's my tender spot! You wanna be bald headed so badly!

My mane spits at the comb, so viciously mauling the crown of my mane.

We're one and the same me and you, my hair and I. I forget that while you are a unit, you define so much of my whole.

And after concluding this rake show, I bind my strands in four sections adjoining them with clips. Mother then starts the ceremony, gilding her hands in stretchy nylon protection

Bringing us to the halfway point in this tale.

Part 2/4:

It is a holy moment; with your right arm you raise the clear amber chemical reagent. Unsheathing it from its plastic Egyptian prison, releasing it to its awaiting honest white no-lye.

With your left, you bear the flat wooden stick, the swordsman who will commune these fine two ingredients.

And then you begin the holy matrimony, a high priestess commencing my journey to pretty.

Gathering my towel tighter at my neck, I mumble quick blessings for my journey up ahead.

Part 3/4:

On the third leg of this odyssey, mother joins the blessed elixir with me, transforming this growing stubborn apprentice into a straight sharp master.

She unclips my hair in the front right hemisphere of our scalp and begins by dividing it again into two.

With half of me held in your safe captivity, your hand reaches to the wooden swordsman in the honest no-lye scooping up a healthy helping.

Total exhale.

The cold white cream is a lollipop to a diabetic child, a fresh rose on a bush.

No, no, I got it. An ice cube on a sun kissed back amidst an equatorial summer. This thick white blessing anoints my strands starting at the ends working and massaging slowly, till surely everything but the growth is covered.

Upon finishing that division, mother moves to the next and repeats this process until it is time to target the true enemy: tough growth.

With my longer strands coated and bound by this transforming white cream, mother now adds just a dollop more to the base of my coarse opponent, weakening her kinky arguments.

In this final face off, I know my loyal no-lye would prove victorious against textured curls and zigzag coils.

Methodically spreading out this white purifier across me, massaging and kneading my tresses like soft dough, I start to doze off because excellence is almost reached

But the itching hasn't started and I've yet to embrace the burn.

Uniting my tresses back in four sections, clipping them apart they return to their beginnings. Removing the nylon protectors, mother produces a clear plastic shroud to crown this pure white offering.

The last holy grail before my rebirth.

About eight minutes pass and I start to feel that ever comforting tingle from deep in my roots.

Like the bull's-eye on a dart board, the crown of my head emerges as the epicenter of tingling.

From that center, tiny ripples of electric current start surging to life; spark by spark in an elaborate agenda to victoriously triumph against the coily natural enemy who has encamped at the roots of my scalp.

Like a monsoon, the too familiar tingling washes into an itchy typhoon causing me to start tilting my head

This way and that; big toe climbing up to the ankle, nervously tapping

Trying not to show discomfort.

Come to life, you straight disciplined locks!

Let no-lye convert your twisted coily sin

Into one fine and divine pretty silky kin

My nonsense fidgeting stops, big toe calming down, neck fixing straight as I embraced the burning of my coils.

At last I could begin to unwind and rest because this great baptizing had admonished every last coily tress.

And when I declared five more minutes, mom nuzzled my hair through this clear film

Nodding her head, approving the decision.

In these last five minutes, I take you all in

Virgin straight tresses

Clad in white, drenched in new blessing

Only so soon will my honesty evoking no-lye

Be rinsed from my head, down the drain

Carrying with it, the pleas of our forgotten coily memory.

And when mother returned, at her promised five minutes

She removed this plastic shrouding to reveal

a newly resurrected head

one with hair as fine as thread, and strong like wool.

Clutching my towel and hopping off the toilet, I walked towards mom. Standing above the tub, preparing water to runneth over my saved hair.

Falling to my knees graciously, the water quenches my crying scalp. Finally, I can rest my eyes because our journey to pretty had reached its end.

Au revoir no-lye, washing off my good haired head

See you again, in three months or whenever coily strands emerge instead of straight on your head.

Part 4/4:

Finally, I stared at my bestie on the box as I'd done a million times before

Tilting my neck at the mirror, brows scrunched in confusion

Shaking my head, my hair moving in slow motion.

It didn't flow like the model, butterfly barrettes tying up her loosely curled tresses

I get it's just for me, but shouldn't it look just like her?

If we both sat on the toilet for the same time

Becoming pretty through honest no-lye

Ignoring the itching embracing the burn

Then they should be undistinguishable

Her hair on my head

Now don't get it twisted, this confusion isn't hate

This confusion isn't disappointment

My confusion is just.

And if it's just for me and just for you

Then it's made for us

To make us be invincible

Looking at the final result, I squeal excitedly

My mother had done it again

Dividing my hair, elaborate braids marked clear
trespassing borders for all strands of newly straight hair
slicked in each section.

In each of those four sections, my happy healthy follicles

Were bound by pink glittery elastics

With happy twin balls clacking loudly when they struck

Halfway down each tress was a color coordinated butterfly
clip

Matching the balls clacking on my scalp.

Together they elevated my self confidence to meet with
God.

Looking at the final result at a different angle, I squeal excitedly

I was absolutely perfect!

My mother had done it again, transforming my tough growth into pretty silky kin.

What is the price of ignorance?

You spend your days in the sun

Never ending summers accompanied with generous blessings from the clouds.

You spend your days eating fruit on a raised hill

You spend your time on the beach shores

You're spending all this time carelessly, ceasing to see how much you really have. What is it costing you?

Because you spend, because you take, you must pay. But how?

You spend your days; sell your hours, trade your seconds, just to buy tomorrow. But at what cost to you?

Your ignorant currency fuels your trips around the sun. You spend your bliss, blissfully! In your forever country summer, you max out your bliss without care- you know no better.

Your ignorant currency, how I wish I had your bliss. How will it refill itself?

It's a bliss spent generously

It lingers long after dreams and midnight moon night colorings- like sand in car mats after beach days.

It suffocates the supposed new day. Is this the tomorrow you bought- one marred in bliss?

Tomorrow is today and now is history.

The sand is too hot and the ocean's waves are frigid and harsh.

Today the sun's beams are too strong, and maybe it's just you, but the rain is overbearing

Maxed Out

Swiping the pleasure that stays stocked inside my credit card.

Wall street journal of green bills exposed and shared with nosy hands, no warmth in palms.

Swiping pleasure, cash back vacations, and withdrawing properties

These are the unimaginable joys that are the consequence of purchase.

Never such a thing as too much, until suddenly there is.

And should that day come, that my happiness maxes out

Swiss funds stoop to Azov lows, I don't know how I'll respond

Except to say that the reader must be malfunctioning.

Here's to the super rich kids who maxed out, but kept going

TV Friendships

Always wanting to be Kim; so that maybe it could be Possible that one day my dark skin is called pretty.

Always wanting to be Rachel and her Friends, but forever I'll be Bébé's kids.

Unwanted, neglected, and destined for a life of solitude.

Jet black locks sit twined on my head, my cornrows plating my scalp. Ready for the helpings of unsavory comments and backhanded condiment compliments that would be served by a salty loud intruder only to be dropped to the floor by my head's quick tilt.

My plate would not be stained with Bébé and Rachel and Bébé and Kim

Bébé and Kim, all the same; the titles don't matter, at least not to me.

My head is held high like a Kim, but unwanted salty helpings follow me everywhere.

Head held high, but not high enough because it's not Possible for Bébé to reach that height.

Staring dead center into my orbs, I flush out my mirror twin.

Using my saline streams, I drown the clamour of negative affirmations that materialize atop the reflective surface before me.

Blessed showers purify the mirrored surface, leaving behind a smiley me and a mirror surface free of vermin.

It's Kuite Possible to be pretty without being Bébé or Kim.

Abort mission... or not

Sitting at the breakfast table enjoying your bacon

Your fingers click & clack admonishing abortion

Blue Skies Mean Death

Blue skies mean death

But there was a time that it meant that if Baba wasn't working, we'd venture to the zoo and pick up roasted smokey nuts nestled in white paper cones.

Blue was my favorite color because it was all around me:

Raspberry frozen slush, fuzzy socks, Puma soccer ball, too scratchy uniform vest.

Blue sky summer days meant sunsets that transcended human capacity for beauty

Blue skies after school meant racing to accomplish your assignments and chores, so that just maybe, you and yours could tussle before dusk.

Chasing clouds with backpacks thumping our vertebrae- we didn't care about our homework at that moment. Dust particles gathered underfoot as we propelled forward, dusting our formerly black loafs in hopes of creating our own clouds to catch the truck to school

Our peers would cheer from their seated positions inside the open window automobile,

"Go, go, go! Come on!" Then finally, with fiery adrenaline propelling my feet, I would latch on to a friendly arm, collapsing flat and out of breath relieved that I did it. And while we jeered and clapped, the expansive blue sky accompanied us as we went to school.

And as I sat at my desk, I waved to our great blue expansive protector begging it to stay open and clear.

Long enough to play football- momentarily forgetting the lessons of the day.

Blue fun filled skies were my friend until they weren't

So soon did I start to hate my wispy white creations in the sky, disguising the fiery death machines that plagued our eastern lands.

Setting fields and humble abodes ablaze in the name of American safety, the blue skies became a star spangled backdrop to death and destruction

When the sky fell atop the roof that day, the clouds didn't cushion my joints as the asphalt collapsed, sending raspberry slushy spilling to the ground.

Yemen

My tears do not hydrate lips nor fill bellies

My tears do not water soil in barren oases

My cries do the opposite of gather cloud clusters and blow them away

My howls threaten rainfall and scatter the clouds

Tears waste water, water we do not have.

It is water we need, not tears.

And still I weep- tirelessly.

Hoping my tears will rain down the rivers of my cheeks and join with the rapids of Alden and carry my pain to the mouths he refreshes.

But so long as I cry, our mouths remain agape and onlookers jeer sympathetically remaining skillfully unhelpful.

Swallow they will my pain, cool at first, clenched, doubled over, they will spit it out.

Tears and water, two sides of the same coin-

Wet, plenty. Plenty of wet tears, not enough water.

We'll get water elsewhere, they say.

NO, I vow.

I weep, sob, howl the clouds away- no water just tears.

Rapids stem from the source of my eyes, cracking lips, cheeks, and all terrain.

Weeping the rapids into cataract dams- broken tears run amuck.

Wet and plenty, tears cascade into their awaiting mouths.

Now they too will cry and their howls will threaten rainfall.

Skyscraper Highs

I'm sorry the circumference of my belly isn't concave
enough for your liking

And that the swollen stomach that signifies

My health, happiness, and nourishment offends your
malnourished palette causing you to frown.

The fullness of my life, reflected in my curves, to you
appears as overindulgence in goodness.

I am de(botched).

And so what, am I not supposed to enjoy the good things
in life?

Be merry on my self centered island, allowing my insides
to fill with

so

much

happiness

that it showers the exterior.

painting me with confidence stripes and dimples of
cheeriness.

Am I supposed to starve myself of what makes me so
sturdy?

Weakening my tower, allowing your jenga trickery to penetrate my high rising confidence

And bring down my esteem to a sad puddle of blocks.

Is that what you want from me?

Do you want me to fall, so graciously from my high point?

Into your arms, weak and breathless

Asking you to define me?

Well if that's what you want, I'll do it just for you.

Except, my tower won't come crashing down.

I'll jump when you're least expecting it

And then I'll let my glorious happiness weigh down your weak arms.

Sadaka

I am not your blessing
Just a problematic answer to a prayer prayed incorrectly
I am not your equal, just a woman in a parallel position
who sees things from this prudent perspective
One dollar offering for one dollar blessings
I'm *the* one dollar, you know?
The one that's given in place of far bigger bills that
command far more promising destinies
You won't donate a decade because to you my worth is
dime
Forget tything twenties, my score to you is sublime.
I know I'm not your blessing because I'm the one dollar
seed you sow only on Sundays to say you gave
something. Right?
One dollar offerings for one dollar blessing because
One polaroid memory crumpled in your paper heart is all
you want in this life with me
I know your change is consistent, but I still hope for a
hundred.
Knowing the only cents you spend are in well meaning
wishing wells to wish us far apart.
Cheaply rewriting the plots of our destiny

Pimp Pimp V.2

Pimp pimp, Amen!

Pimp, pimp, Amen!

Pimp blue suit always preaching 'bout salvation

On your pulpit you stand, erect and sturdy

Like your black rule book of conduct.

Speaking the wonderful consequences of trickery to you

You declare that we're His, but we're yours for the making. The making of moving mountains, parting seas, appeasement of generous drought.

All that can only happen once you've come to his flower bed of green and planted your contribution

A sort of tithe.

Pimp blue suit always preaching 'bout salvation

Because pimp blue is the color of the tides of blessings that will surely flow into your life like water

Once you accept the pimp blue charity.

And now your blessed pimp blue waves, will water the green nutritious peacock pastures that grow from this newly pregnant land.

Dams are destroyed, waves are summoned, and typhoons
seize at your entrance!

You boast fervently, blessing foaming at the mouth.
Salivating at the thought of your kind charity

Pointing and stomping, up and down and up and down

At the results of your work

Evidence two pews deep, each side of the aisle. Four full
pews of blessings as evidence

How could it be anything but?

So willingly we do, line up to be planted into your
peacock green garden

Awaiting pimp blue showers.

Sunday

I want a Sunday morning love

One that outlives Saturday night passions

and lingers like the rays of sun in every corner of the
room.

Louder than Saturday's secret, I want to be the cover
of your Sunday paper.

Letting the sweet words of your proclamation caress
and envelope me whole

Stamping your kisses in the corners of my lips

You'd seal our love and send it out into the world.

But I know the truth about me and you

I'll forever be below the fold, shamefully tucked
behind the mundane weather report

While proudly, your headshot gazes purposefully- the
only reason people picked up the paper.

Pixie Dust

Am I really your magic, or just a one trick show?

The bunny in your magic hat, popping up only when cued.

One way ticket to wonderland.

A bell that sits at the corner of your isolated Neverland desk, unnoticed and rarely visited.

Am I that bell?

Resounding my sharp tune only at the tinkering of another's wrist.

I am the neglected license in the crook of your wallet.

Only proudly claimed and shown in the coincidental meetings with crooked cops and bemused bartenders.

You say I'm your golden magic,

Sprinkled atop any and every thing

To make it tenfold sweeter entirely.

You say my magic gilds all it touches, but is that a bad thing?

Does my Midas magic embarrass you?

Is it because even a little amount of it absorbs a single sunny ray and deflects it in every which way?

My little is a lot

And I guess too much for you.

Is it my shine that forces you to conjure a stifling cloak?

To shroud my light and smother before it catches a pupil.

You like me in controlled doses.

Because my reflected shine you can't control, but a ray of light you can.

And gather you do clouds of dismay and shame

To stop the beaming sun

From feeding me its magic light.

You like my shine, but only on arctic winter days

Where I do nothing but give light without warmth.

You don't let me have summer because then I'd be reprieve from arctic memory.

PC Compatible?

HTML your love is javascript coded

I'll need a crypt of crunching code to program any real meaning

Seeing in shades of 0's and 1's, never twoned in with your heart's four chambers, three of which do not belong to me

You open Windows to refresh our Microsoft wordings hoping your newly installed virus lies crash this new tab- which you're paying for

My Chrome heart can't download anymore shame

And an Apple a day doesn't keep my worries away.

I have no real way of Delling with your Alien language

Growing Rosetta Stonefaced annoyed at your insistent Nike advertisements saying you just had to do it

You are the king of this, so you'll always have it your way

That's why you never internet explore my endless emotional filings.

I don't want to program my python poison to paint my point across

So please, please

Just print me a copy of the fax you keep hidden in your heart's cache

Your love isn't blind anymore

If I break your heart, I'm not sorry.

I won't apologize for knowing you so well

for knowing which buttons to push to shoot us to the depths of hell.

If it makes you feel better, I was thinking of you when I came.

To the conclusion that this would be your last straw- this final crescendo, nothing could redeem me

And I thought of you again soon after because as good as it felt, she'll never be you. but I'm still not sorry

I'm not sorry for taking all that love and using it to build me up.

I refuse to apologize for all the secret laughs and hands held.

Raising you to a new standard- I was the necessary teacher

Whose shrewd love upgraded you for all relationships after me.

If I held you back, at least I held you close

Transferring all this loneliness inside me, nursing it between us

Bulking nimble skeletons into muscular fixtures.

White women are just women

White women are just women; their whiteness a blank
canvas anointed by a base of eternal protection and
freedom of unchecked discovery. Canvas only collecting
color by the wrist of their hand

Master ventriloquist, no strings ever attached

Canvas immune to the narrative of outside forces.

Only bleeding by the demand of your spongy brush.

Not knowing what it's like to be tethered by strings you'll
never recognize

Spending days and hours bound to the design of others.
You see my erratic canvas being painted by a limp wrist

being tugged in every direction except by the one my heart
yearns, and you stare with confusion at this marred canvas
in comparison to your pristine one.

Frightened by this sight, you pack your canvas up and away
from this ugly interference, even though you know it could
never paint your canvas

Momentarily, you consider inviting limp wrist woman

But the way her heart's not in it

Just doesn't suit your purified path of letting emotion and self be your ultimate guide.

Why can't limp wrist woman catch up?

White women are just women because they are blank like the canvas they are afforded and prepared like their tool laden studio.

A canvas worthy of Rafael

Paints that would make Picasso blush

Pens so thin and fine that even Seurat and Signac would make a point to praise their refinery.

With a blank canvas and unbound wrist

They are allowed to express and discover each hue and medium in the spacious studio that is their life.

No one is there, imposing on their creativity

Stifling their expression

Critiquing the shades of fuchsia and neutral fawns

Reporting that those forms are not them.

No tongue reprimands and belittles in sweet suggestion

that it is not you who knows your heart

but rather them, because they have dissected and torn it apart

each chamber invaded and valve torn off its hinges.

To be white and woman is to have unscathed potential that will be accepted at all points of this thing called life.

You may rebel

May you be submissive

You may be unapologetic

May you be delicate

You may be demanding

My penny spins heads and tails

Yours coins copper into nickel.

Black women are void

Black women are void of womanhood because they are Black first, woman second, then human third.

That is the order of my humanity. By the time you get to human, Black has nullified and femininity has carnaged authentic delicacy from her most divine.

Black first, woman second, human last.

Human last, Black first

Meaning my fruits will be bared long before I'm ready.

The fruits of my art will be pillaged as I work never allowing me to conceive mastery.

Paint still running- *not fast enough*- pastel freshly powdered, my canvas is torn from my grip to be presented for bashful jeering and unfair scorn.

How dare they mock my unfinished Rome?

But I can't say that because I haven't the time to spare for such words. As soon as a canvas leaves my grip, clock's hand slaps. Causing red stain to paint my skin canvas, reminding me who I bleed from.

I hear you complain about your studio, pointing out Signac flaws and Rafael shortcomings

All the while I paint in the hallway. Ceiling leaking, brushes missing, and canvas empty.

You can afford to complain because when your easel stands stable, paints sit stagnant, and you've won custody over your canvas, you can spend your money on words instead of things.

I'd like to stand surefooted and form a conjecture, but I can't.

I'm pneumonic from ceiling water drips, and my legs are as sturdy as chopsticks in a foreigner's grip.

If my currency was so refined then I would command white girl problems.

Rinsing them in humanity and commanding empathy showers to wash over my petalless plantings.

Showing that they too can be beautiful, with the proper care. But I am not white, my problems don't melt like snow.

Like Frosty's eyes, they're resilient coal lumps.

Staying way past winter, surviving in spring, just to be charred in summer grills.

Compromise

Really, my nigga?

$3/5^{th}$ of a nigga, you not even whole

always asking me to compromise something for you
feeble ass nigga

You're a fraction of a man

Never giving just demand

And on my pedestal, yes I stand arms raised to the
heavens

I refuse to hold your hand!

Cause when that hand gets to holding

When my wrist holds out that whimsical love,
empathy sweets, a salad of knowledge or whatever it
be

Your steely iron grip pours a scalding hot molding

Over my wrist, encasing my palms, a goodbye to
pink manicures and free mobility

Tricked into your steel captivity

My hand is now yours with all it was holding.

Goodbye whimsical love, I nurtured you so long

Au revoir ability to be sweet to myself, bitterness will
nest the cavernous ruin you've left

And knowledge of discernment, when will I learn to trust
me again?

I don't know, but this I do

When me and you are through

You'll have escaped with my generous hand

My truths belonging to you

Reddington

Wisdom is wasted on the old and withering

While youth is squandered on the young, too young to know what they want

Still counting steps carefully like timid toddler kindergarteners.

Wisdom is wasted on the old, stuck on a train never stepping off

While gallivanting youth with upside down maps move merrily to incorrect destinations

Happiness intact, hopping from platform to platform ready to challenge young afternoons

While wise all knowing elders watch safely in steely carriages

Knowing adventure is not always worth the price of third degree sunburns

What life have they left?

Praying to God about shoulda and woulda as often as granny bakes cookies

A life of maybe, coulda, shoulda belongs to those who have time to rewrite their narratives before rolling end credits begin to summarize life's movie plots

Youth belongs to withering trees who need distraction from the pain of deteriorating limbs and ache of falling leaves.

Only youth can begin to pluck bullet shell casings shot from life's 9 mm. bullet clips.

Youth is the only substitute for love lost.

Springtime Deception

Spring brings new beginnings and life renews

Vivid pink blossoms awaken, reminding me of the time we met

Snow and wind gave me blues, then spring came and brought me you

The time we spent I will never forget.

Vivid pink blossoms awaken, reminding me of the time we met

When you kept getting hospitalized that should have been a sign.

The time we spent, I will never forget.

Your melodies and laugh echo in my head; frozen in time.

When you kept getting hospitalized that should have been a sign.

Your words with me always, continue to ring true

Your melodies and laugh echo in my head; frozen in time.

My strokes on the ivory keys, I hope they reach you

Your words with me always, continue to ring true

Snow and wind gave me blues, then spring came and brought me you

My strokes on the ivory keys, I hope they reached you

Spring brings new beginnings and life renews

Kinky

Let me be kinky, don't refine me like my edges

The entrance to my crowned garden, they flourish my puffy hedges

Don't bind me to your 3c tresses. Let me be real, I 4c what you're telling

You want this tropical garden to be vanilla like the ice caps

But I won't allow it. My edges will be rich and thick like the palm leaves that canopy my Amazonian oasis.

My edges will flow this way and that, like the river Euphrates

Unconstrained and free, embarking untouched frontier. A circumference of truth

I don't wish to be vanilla. Refined and unfulfilling; ice caps, glaciers, creatures all the same

Refined and frozen by arctic Eco Styling

It all looks the same, and that brings me great pain.

My hands will become, the ultimate rigger

Tying my healthy tresses into sturdy straight-back ropes

Protected and bound, suspended on my head

My great Samsonite tresses

And my free healthy edges encrusting my crown

Flourishing and growing because I didn't let Delilah's
Eco Styling cut them down.

Carol's daughter, Uncle Hicks, Aunty Camille

Please I've had enough of your goopy stick gab.

I want my edges to be coily, kinky, and truthful

So I'll say it once again

Don't refine me; take me kinky like my edges

Gamerboy

You play with my heart X's and O's

Tic Tac Toe

Tic is for the ticking time seconds you stole from me.

Sweetest thief I had come to know

Tac is how you attached yourself on everything I had come to know.

Your lingering scent dancing on the wind of a busy street causes my heart to ache and my eyes to wander.

Trees of nature doing their best to outshine the shy hazel flecks in your luring guise-

Filling my lungs with air while always leaving me breathless.

Sulci of my brain rewired and disfigured to the familiar shape of your name

And oh, how you made my eyes spin off their axes

Arms interwoven, lips locked, noses colliding.

Steady melody we created; one of one, like no other.

So you see, in this game of X's and O's

I crossed my heart and hoped to love

And there you Orrived.

Scales

Do you

Remember

Mi

Fa all the

Songs I wrote with you?

Late nights spend with your hands imprinted into my neck, safe in your embrace. Because

Time was cheap, we got drunk on wasting it.

Do you regret it?

Confidence for two, please

I'm not hungry for you, I'm full of myself and have sides to go along.

My stomach, selective with what we'll receive, peers out at the dish that sits before us

I uncover the first dish presented before me

to unveil a crude poison.

You stand behind your dish, a proud smirk on your face

Your love, you proclaim acknowledging the dish with a flourish of the wrist.

It is -physically- off putting and foul

Scaly in appearance, coarse in texture, the sludge drips down your ladle menacingly as you attempt to force it on me, but not before I jerk my plate back.

I'm full of my love, and need none of yours.

Yours is foreign, uninviting, and malnutritious

This love is the same as yours, you weakly crow into my ears

No! This placebo love, you must want to make me sick

I'm overflowing with joy

Boldness boiling, brimming off the top

My passion simmers slowly and trusty at the fiery depths of my soul

brewing my love, keeping it ablaze

And as my love sizzles and bubbles, it starts to take its true form.

The flames rise high- licking and stitching wounds you have inflicted with your cruel inadequacy.

And it is in my passionate flame that I am reborn.

Your once venomous words, now ashen lie dead and fruitless like their origin. I emerge from the flames to walk atop you, so that through my soles you may feel the presence of truth.

My broiled complexion dripping in embers

Browned and perfected by the ever burning pit like the truest mother earth.

This is my love.

So you see, you could never serve me truly, because I'm full
off my love and want second helpings

and will ignite even the crudest of offerings to keep my
love burning

To each their own

Happiness is avocado and pineapples, bound together
with bumblebees' amber love child.

Its signature drink is ginger tea with a squeeze of
zealous lemon- cleansing and enriching

Smells like peach sangria

Dresses in free flowing garments and knitwear

It's surrounded by lush green forests and consumes the
fruits of her labor on the land she lives on

Happiness is vulnerability; the only walls that stand are
those in her home

where they protect and lay foundation.

It exists naturally as the wind and the sun. Free, yet fixed
and sturdy

For all to see and engage

Helen

I have a fear of happiness

Terrified of intimacy

Disgusted by warm embrace

Unsoothed by tender touch

Confused about pinky taps

Indifferent to lingering eye contact

All because I think I'm hard to love

Loving me is easy though

You just need a bulletproof soul

That is built for withstanding the climb

To the peak of my high Troy walls.

Yes, it can be slightly unguarded.

Only if I'm left alone with you for so long

Which I try not to allow.

When the archers' bows and arrow fall limp

And the gallant swordsmen get distracted

That is when my limestone blocks start to fall and crumble.

Susceptible to your gentleness

Captivated by your attention to detail.

I then remember the pang of arrows in the flesh

The pain of sword cuts

The absence of strength in my limbs

That result from lifting my limestone blocks up again

Not consenting to the rearrangement that comes with your love.

But as Artemis wrists begin to go limp

And Achilles heels weaken

My limestone blocks become more generous to your love laden palm

Allowing your artistic rearranging to deliberately pluck

Every swordsman and archer from their post

Filling their empty slots with our newly emerged happiness.

We Are The Sun

It was the best of times and it was the worst of times. As we stood in serenade of his song, voices coming together to form harmonious riffs, his hand gripping the microphone the other occupied with my cheek, our happiness felt displaced. Here we were living at the end, foes and friends alike rising and falling like a steady tide, yet all we could see was the sand. We sit on this beach of finite possibility, and instead of letting the fear and worry that loom in colliding waves wash over us, we dig our feet into sandy promise, allowing panic and anxiety to be planted underfoot where it can cause no harm. On our ever doomed beach, we erect sandcastle societies to hold onto our individual grains of truth. So that one day, if the tides did come crashing in, they would know we were here. By the resistance of sandy walls and our union of truths standing as protectors of the city, the wanton waves would know the people they're striking down. On this doomed sandy beach, we celebrate so desperately the tomorrows we'll never see. Sanitizing the air with spritzes of infectious laughter, we would create a musical atmosphere so loud that the chiming of our echoes would fill the land and inherit the sea long after our departure. Acknowledging this apocalyptic fantasy to be true, we stand calmly in the queue. Awaiting our impending finale, letting song be our chosen language. So as we gather around our circle of song, friends yelling memorized lyrics, your cheek pressed in my palm, I allow this moment of existence to stamp itself in the timeline of my life. So that way if we're forced to run, up, up and away from what we've built, I can fill my bag for the next life with the organic truth I experienced living among you.

Library

The genre of my humanity is black, and I'm just another book on the shelf.

But no one cares to read me.

I sit fixed and unmoving as curious curling fingertips curve over my spine.

Raising paper goosebumps from my tightly wound binding

Lingering long enough to blink away my champion Title.

Brisky, as to not burden the mind with the assignment of learning my name.

All the peaches & mangoes I would sell for

you

In my turbulent Red Sea, your orange channel pruned and soothed my deepest worries

I was enamoured by the divine way you parted my waters, no longer afraid of the wildlife that flourish and swim underneath

My shy wrist tentatively springs
awake to touch your ever calming
ripples.

Wading over

each

individual

finger tip

this new peaceful revelation cleanses my redy worries that seas me captive

Alone now, walking at the floor of my pebbled Red Sea, my feet pound the clementine orange path you painted.

Excitedly, escaping from my former self; free from the red shackles that so desperately wanted to seas me.

She would make me her personal footstool, this tethered woman who I used to know

Each alluringly sweet step taken across this wise orange channel only reminds me that I must embark on this mission.

A journey is a gift that is not presented to judgmental pyramids

Erected in vain, they stand above me in the distance. Marinating spite at their eternal foundations; never able to unsheathe the jewels and shed sarcophagus

To begin a new eternity for themselves

Because of their inability to unbecome their formers' desire, they send out waves of arrows and darts

To strike me dead so that my bleeding red will seas me in place draining me of the clementine gift that I amour so heavily

Sweet, zesty, rich in texture this now sweet life is my new favorite marmalade

Each peel suspended in your wise orange amber

Feeding my hangry doubts, transforming them into nutritious affirmations.

I have spent nine years on this orange lightning strip

Being charged with unflinching questions and paying with gentle vulnerability

The road to Sierra Leone is a long one indeed, but so long as I don't stray from my greatest orange gift

I too can channel a color of my own and add meaning to my pink matter.

Wicked smaht

Maple leafs and stop signs, who's copying who?

Orange pumpkin carvings mirroring orange Dunkin D's.

Abundant winter showers, leave roofs shrouded in white,
like Miami in the eighties.

Serene lakes and bodies of water bordering on any and
every landscape.

Semi aquatic mermaids, citizens of our fake Atlantis.

Over here, trees plant seeds of mischievous climbing into
the brains of watchful children.

Tawny sturdy tree limbs send out invitations of ascendance
to onlookers, daring all to familiarize themselves with the
trees' anatomy from root to tip.

The lonely leaf at the peak of this raised bush waves back
and forth, back and forth.

A checkered flag for those who dare to take the trek.

Crisp air present in all shuffled seasons:

Salty in the summer breeze

Whip sharp in arctic blizzard,

Smoky and rich in autumn fires

Pollinated and blossoming in spring.

Coming of Age: From Smarties to Backwoods

You Remained Constant

I'll never forget the first time you came, because unlike the others you stayed.

Held captive by salt and vinegar aisles, I became one with the scratch tickets that itched at my back- never satisfying the scratch and scream from my wallet. Linoleum tiles you and yours greeted gleefully and hopped over energetically, only continued to serve as a reminder of the Dorito laden prison I was confined to. Each tile you clamour atop energized, without looking back, only representative of days of freedom I'll never be refunded. Everyday in this establishment is spent bartering in chips and coins, the forgettable side character in my protagonist customers. In these four walls you were free- unsupervised to pick whatever snacks and poisons you wanted knowing only to throw away evidence of your sinful indulgence blocks before your arrival home. I am the holder of all shameful secrets from pickle juice and honey bun pairings to Smirnoff in coffee cups. These four walls represent pleasure and ultimate satisfaction to all who ring and enter this bell jar- Sodom and Gomorrah, an oasis of indulgence- and it is me who enables, in this symbiotic relationship. Crippling and debauching their lives, I accept their donations to keep these lights on.

Teal Marlboros or red Kamels, which to stock? Palming both tobacco products in hand, I weighed the

122

two as if to choose a healthier alternative. Smiling to myself, I choose the red Kamels simply because the latter contained menthol. I place the toxic box back in my pocket for safe keeping, but not before scrunching my nose in disapproval at the habit and the foul scent. Idly, I start stocking the red Kamels and as I pack the last one in place, the bell above the door jingles merrily and in comes you.

You weren't alone though, you were in the company of three other four foot gnomes under the protective eye of a responsible teenager. A little boy-freckle adorned arms and healthy cheeks- swimming in an extroverted cherry red vest and true blue shorts led your menacing quartet. At his side stood a lanky gap toothed girl; healthy cheeks to frame her lantern blonde hair, wearing pink and green plaid shorts and a torso clad in black. The third was a sun kissed boy- skin amber like desert sands- with jet black hair and a matching Disney ensemble. And you were at his side chatting up an exciting tale with your arms motioning freely. Two perfect space buns bound together by playful beady barrettes sat on your proud head and when you smiled, you revealed one gap at the front of your mouth. To combat the heat you decided to strap on a jean denim dress- a singular pocket stitched in vibrant cardinal was sewn on your chest, ready to hold all the little treasures a little girl may find. Underneath you sported a white tee and long leggings, on your feet white laced up kicks.

I chuckled fondly internally- this outfit was surely chosen with love and held no regard to the attacks of the merciless sun. You and your minions dispersed in the aisles, like organized assassins, you covered ground and hunted down the snacks and treats with unforgiving focus.

"Hey, we don't have enough money for that Sam! Put it back, remember when we counted the money we said we'll all give three dollars." Began the lantern headed blonde, revealing the identity of Mickey Mouse's biggest fan. His face scrunched in dissatisfaction at their broke dilemma. Sending a longing sorrowful glance at the bag of hot chips, he started with his head down to reunite the bag with its almost forgotten family. To stop this tragic farewell, you tugged his arm and whispered in his ear what had to be a solution to his issue, because his doe eyes sparked back with life and he nodded fervently. Snatching the bag from his parental grip, you marched towards the counter dinging the bell that was in front of you even though you saw me behind the counter.

"Excuse me, but can we please get this bag of hot chips for free please? My friend really wants it because it's his favorite snack in the whole entire world, and it'll be really sad if we leave without it because he loves it so much just because we don't have money for it. Plus, it's only $1.50 so you won't lose a lot of money by giving it to us."

She so candidly inquired; she then grabbed the boy's arm and pulled him beside her, "Can you please make him smile today? His birthday was last week too, you didn't know us then, but consider it a gift." As if on cue, he humbled his head to the ground and framed his black rounded eyes square in mine. Shock electrocuted

124

me entirely, causing me to pause and ponder this demand.

Never had an attempt to manipulate me been so brazen and unflinching- by a child at that. The sheer confidence and composure in this little girl; clipped and concise, she laid bare her dilemma and how I could be of service in fixing it, and so tactfully outlined the consequence of my actions: being the reason a little boy would be sad today. Simultaneously, she also gave me a hint of my reward: I could be the reason a little boy flashes a spicy smile. In even acknowledging my $1.50 shortcomings, she understood that this was a somewhat taboo request. And I couldn't help but fixate on the fact that she made no promises of refunding the $1.50 at a later date. It was based on her crafty nature that I created my answer. You smiled carefully, raising your eyebrows to summon a final verdict from my judicial standing at the counter.

"Because you were so polite and reasonable, of course you can have the chips for free, and here's an airhead for each of you. But this won't happen all the time. Understand?" I declare to my awaiting audience.

"I told you it would work!" She muttered excitedly, reuniting the chips with their awaiting consumer; I knew I wasn't supposed to hear it, but I smiled nonetheless- clever child. I rang up all your items and when it was time to pay the total, you handed me the precise $12.27.

With your three dollars, you purchased a raspberry Snapple and a salty sweet bag of chips. Freckle boy bought a big burst and hot chips, lantern blonde acquired a singular drum of ice cream, and Mickey's protégé accompanied his free hot chips with fruit punch, and a shareable pouch of skittles. After our transaction was completed you all started your way to the door towards your teen protectorate, synchronized black bags swaying happily with each step. But you hesitated at the door and turned back around for the counter.

"Thank you so much, especially for the airheads. We appreciate it a lot." Your head bobbled as you breathed out your thanks, and before I could shape my lips to acknowledge my deed and compliment your manners, you rushed out the door. You heeded my instructions though, because every Saturday -for three years- when you came to tithe your $12.27, you never attempted to manipulate me and you religiously washed down your savory chips with the refreshing raspberry Snapple. And in those three years, I watched you beg and plead your ever loved denim dress to grow with you and not out; until one day, I noticed you had made your quell with puberty and stopped wearing it as the dress turned shirt it had become.

You came with your friends on Saturdays, but on weekday mornings it was you who awoke the sleeping linoleum aisles- feet slapped excitedly, alarming the fridge of your prowling presence. You reached the chilled jaws, grabbing a coral shaded bottle containing delicious strawberry milk to start your day. It was pastel pink like the backpack you had in years two through four of our encounters. The Saturday afternoon gang dissolved their contract with me after year three of us knowing each other, but I remained your steady dealer to your weekday fixings. As expected, your candor and wit were the condiments of our discussion, always a sprinkle of something woefully honest. After a while, I just let you help yourself to whatever on your way to school because the consequence you hinted at upon our initial meeting always lingered in my head.

Make him smile today. The mantra that resounded in my head, like the bell that notified me of your arrival at 7:56 AM daily. While most days were filled with short lived banter, there were some where silence rang you up and the receipt was understanding. This approachable silence increased as you grew older, but I didn't mind it one bit.

In year seven of our encounters though, you came in on a Sunday, which was a rare occurrence. You had headphones nestled in your ears, so I knew this was going to be a silent day. Before you though, a man had entered the store wading through aisles locating his tokens. I pulled my phone out to pass a few moments while you two strangers delighted in your pleasure. Finally having located his materials, the man approached the counter kindly greeting the tiles with his sneakers. Before me laid a spearmint pack of gum and a bottle of tequila.

"Two of those as well, please." His gilded fingers gestured at a particularly vibrant pack of cigarillos hanging behind me. As I turned my back to retrieve the berry flavored Backwoods, the door to this bell jar jingled, but I paid it no mind- yet again welcoming another client. Without missing a beat, the man confirms his maturity while inserting his card into the reader. Sandwiching the two packs atop his gum and liquor, I bag his belongings and send him on his way with a smile and half sincere well wish. After that transaction, I looked out into the store and I was shocked to see it bare. The ringing door.

Then it hit me. You didn't grab anything from the shelves to satisfy your never expiring free voucher. You never come in without at least a wave to signal your departure, so I peered out the congested window pane and watched the exchange occur before me, bewilderment holding me hostage.

The man whom I sold the berry flavored backwoods handed you the package. Your fingers lingered on his palms- long enough for him to notice, abrupt enough to not endanger you. Clearly aroused by this brief manipulation from a young woman, he flashed a tight lipped grin. All semblance of stress leaving his body and rising hot and embarrassed in the tips of his ears. Although this interaction lasted for only ten seconds, I saw you as more than the girl who couldn't survive a day without strawberry milk. You were a woman in your own right, and to see such an honest intentional interaction of power and womanizing, I understood that my judgments held to you in that moment were unfair and naive.

After all, did you not successfully manipulate me upon introduction? Wasn't it you who branded my daily mantra in my lifestyle? How many times had I batted my lashes and drizzled my guise to get away with a parking ticket? Purposefully lingered my gaze at the mouth of a man to get him to conform to my will? As the man walked back to his car -hand twitching with confidence- you turned around and met my peering eyes. We paused time for a moment, holding each other's gaze before you held up the honey berry backwoods and flashed a wink.

"Thank you." you mouthed, and then we resumed with our days respectively. You rushed to your car and left me to be the keeper of salty, sweet days of freedom.

Lamentations 1:9

Her filthiness clung to her skirts as she surrendered her white sullied cloth at her ankles with the world watching her glory grow former with each passing day.

Swaying seductively, you bare your upright breasts and figure perfection to onlooking crowds

Freeing yourself from past sin, entering new, you step out and over your sullied drapes awaiting applause and the

Oohs and aahs that unwillingly quip from every mouth, rinsing the room with inhumane flattery giving you what you were looking for.

Is the noise for you or your glory? Once two sides of one face, a chasm now sits where the latter existed

Is the noise for you or your glory? Fading faint and nimble with each day, your once commanding Jerusalem was a threat.

Where confidence was once erected, defeat and insecurity stand pathetically. On shaken foundation, your flaccid playdough monument showcases the true failure of your queenly ability to protect what's yours.

Desperately, tears run amuck, attempting to summon anointed waters underfoot to drown out your orchestrated clamour of failure.

You are not power, glory does not become you; it is a gift that you were born without, and you refused to accept this fate.

So you searched and searched, desperately looking for glorious power.

A bed with supporting sheets instead of a sleeping bag; something to sleep on top of and not inside- fitting for a self-appointed shallow queen who refuses to venture into deeper waters.

One who prefers the imprisonment of sandbar's entrapment of beauteous vanity

To the freedom that comes with becoming a student at the school of acceptance.

Because its GPS coordinates reside in always changing water waves; unpredictability demanding apprentices to become masters through submission to teacher's unguided instruction of crashing waters.

They are true power because of their inability to remain in steady beat; the depth of their unpredictability whipping away shallowness, demanding boundless inquisition to materialize in the former's place.

One by one, overripe fruits of frivolous vanity voluntarily fall off overflowed branches.

Only through naked vulnerability can wondrous gifts of confidence and power begin to bud.

But you do not want to be naked and vulnera-*afraid*- so you will continue your quest on sandy shores.

Happy to plant your soles atop power's placebo twin; burying your toes in sand's endless grains of fake truth.

You search for that blanket of power to cover up fear's yellow piss that stains sheets you sleep on.

Power to protect fluffy pillows of pathetic and shallow.

Power heard of your stubbornness and she decided to fuck you out your sturdy paper palace.

Upon entry: Your nobility stripped, divinity denied, confidence expired, just like that.

Her steps are noiseless, making it impossible to predict next steps.

You became aware of her presence, not when your sacred white shrouding fell soundlessly to the floor, but when your nipples pruned and realized you were vulnerable and exposed. Afraid at last.

To protect her peaceful pristine palace, Power commands your pathetic tears to flow upward and silences your cries to telepathic realms.

Matriculated from their school of acceptance, students turned masters jeer and whoop, at the result of rejecting their master's teaching.

Willingly this time, Oohs and aahs fall from their lips at the sight of an archaic mess so beautifully packaged.

Figure perfection and erect breasts mean nothing when they uphold no truth.

White cloth only drapes skeletal framework, it does not fatten up nimble limbs. Only exaggerates the weakness of the structure.

So I ask again, is the noise for you or your former glory?

Do they jeer for your befallen status or the uncovering of such a horrid site? In the quips, is there even a cleft of respect and wonder striking their vocals?

The noise blanketing the room, rises to a deafening high as you finally resign your cloth to the floor, at last.

So you dance for Power, bit by bit becoming nothing but a woman arrested.

Acknowledgements

First and foremost, I would like to thank God for giving me this gift of gab and it is through His grace that this project was able to go as far as it did. Thank you to my family for taking me seriously, praying for me, and always encouraging me. Thankful to my spiritual elders for walking with me, may God continue to sustain us. Special thanks to Natalie Sebowa; from sharing weak lines to conversations at dawn, you have been the only person to see this project from its genesis. Your honesty is much appreciated. Vivian Njuguna, the best cousin and friend I could ask for; I thank God for solidifying our place in each other's life. Thank you Anjali, your illustrations brought this book to life. Thank you Maryam, your images transformed this project to a new level. Thank you Karen Fortier; your intelligence, unflinching honesty, and ability to make me confront myself have been a great luxury to my life. Fellow author, Masada Jones thank you for reviewing, *Just For Me*. Ruth Ogembo and Eric Johnson for being trusting confidants, no words can encapsulate what you both mean to me; thank you forever. Thank you Rachelle for being my first reader. Thank you to everyone who let me interview and photograph them; thank you for treating this project with care and respect. Lastly, I thank myself for juggling so much and consistently meeting my demanding expectations.

About the Author

All the Peaches & Mangoes I Would Sell For You is Ivy Prints and Ivy Ngugi's debut novel. Keep up with Ivy Prints by subscribing to The Vine Newsletter at ivyprintsllc.com and following the company on Instagram @ivyprintsllc. Catch up with Ivy Ngugi on her blog and podcast at thenoablog.com and follow the blog on Instagram @thenoablog.

Purity, by Maryam Rose (@afadedrose on Instagram).

Ivyprintsllc.com

CPSIA information can be obtained
at www.ICGtesting.com
Printed in the USA
BVHW031314140921
616742BV00008B/62